Poems by J.R. Solonche

David Robert Books

Published by David Robert Books
P.O. Box 541106
Cincinnati, OH 45254-1106

ISBN: 9781625494689

Poetry Editor: Kevin Walzer
Business Editor: Lori Jareo

Visit us on the web at www.davidrobertbooks.com

Books by J.R. Solonche

Then Morning
The Architect's House
God
The Eglantine
Alone
The Dreams of the Gods
The Book of a Small Fisherman
Leda
It's about Time
Around Here
The Lost Notebook of Zhao Li
Coming To
Life-Size
The Five Notebooks of Zhao Li
Selected Poems 2002-2021
Years Later
The Dust
A Guide of the Perplexed
For All I Know
The Moon Is the Capital of the World
Piano Music
Enjoy Yourself
The Time of Your Life
The Porch Poems
To Say the Least
A Public Place
True Enough
If You Should See Me Walking on the Road
I, Emily Dickinson and Other Found Poems
The Jewish Dancing Master
Tomorrow, Today and Yesterday
In Short Order
Invisible

Table of Contents

Old

I am old, I know.
I do not need to be told,
but tell me anyway,
for I want to hear you say,
"Solonche, look at that deep brow,
at that gray hair, at that back bowed
under those seventy-six
years." I want to hear you say,
"Mister, you're all done with sex."
I want to hear you say,
"But don't worry, old man,
you'll soon be done being old.
You'll soon enough be cold."
Oh, yes, I am old. Humor me.

The Song

When I was a child, I read
a book called *The Song.* It
was about a boy about my
age who loved to sing, but
no one wanted to hear him
sing. His mother, his father,
his brother, his sister, his
classmates, none of them
wanted to hear him sing. So
he would go for walks in the
woods behind his house and
sing to himself. One day while
walking on an unfamiliar path,
he discovered a tree standing
by itself. It was small, not much
taller than a sapling. In fact, it
was his height exactly. He sat
down next to it and began to sing
his song. Suddenly, an amazing
thing happened. The tree started
to grow. It grew and grew until it
was the tallest tree in the forest.

It was a very strange ending to a very strange story, but to me the only ending that made any sense. I wanted to give the book to my daughter, but I've no idea what became of it.

My Life

I passed the window
and glanced in the glass
and saw myself as if
for the first time in my life,
and it was a face I would never
in my life want to live with
and never want to be loved.

I Know It's Too Soon

I know it's too soon,
but I pulled them up
anyway from the pots,
the half dead flowers
along with the dead and
threw them together into
the tall weedy grass where
they can still be flowers
if they insist.

Seeing Me Sitting

Seeing me sitting
outside waiting for my
financial advisor to stop
by to advise me of my
finances, the sun says,
 "Solonche, you foolish
old man, here, come nap
upon my golden lap."

It Is Difficult

It is difficult, difficult
to be outside on such
a day of such a sun
and not want to do
what Caedmon did,
write a hymn to it, that
sun on that day back when.
Oh, it is difficult not to begin.

The Cruelty Of Exactitude

It's the mind's right
to expect faultlessness.
"Picture it," it demands,
and although you can't,
try as you might,
you still will blame only your hands.

Sundown

Go down the stairs at sundown.

Go down the road at sundown.

Go down the valley at sundown.

Go down to the oak tree at sundown.

Go down on your knees at sundown.

Go down to the depth of your silence at sundown.

Go down to the heart of your soul at sundown.

Jim And I Were Talking About

Jim and I were talking about
sex. I don't remember the last
time I had sex, I said. I do, he
said. Gee, it must have been
really recently, I said. No. It was
years ago, he said. Then it must
have been pretty good if you
still remember it, I said. It was.
I think it was the best I ever
had, he said. Well, I'm glad
I don't remember the last time
I had sex. I'm sure it was lousy,
I said. Do you remember the
first time? he said. Yeah, I do.
Doesn't everyone? I said. And?
he said. And that was even worse,
I said. Yeah, like everyone, he said.
Yeah, Hugh Heffner's fault, I said.
For me it was the other guy, he said.

Poem For A Difficult Future

The future will be difficult,
he said. He was a scientist,
an expert on global warming,
so he knew what he was
talking about. Prepare for it,
he said. So I prepared this
poem for a difficult future.
I'm a poet, so I know what
I'm talking about. Remember
this when the difficult future
becomes the difficult present.
"Gaia, Mother, Goddess of Earth,
forgive us, forgive us for taking
the easy way out. Amen."

Expression

Give me your true
face, the one

you use first thing
in the morning

when the dream
begins to fade away.

Make me your mirror.
Make me your mirror,

and I will tell you,
and I will tell you

just how fair I am,
just how far away,

just how far away
you are from you.

Longing

I, too, know it in
my bones, feel it
bleed from my eyes,
the cruel blindness
worse than blindness,
the blindness that lets
you see that for which
you long and that alone.

Old

Old and older than
and oldest among
and the young (Bless
their hearts!) shall live
to regret all they say
about us.

Confession

When I was a teenager,
I envied my Catholic
friends, Mike McTeague
and Anthony Grazioli,
who went to church every
week to be absolved of
their sins while I, the Jew,
had to hold all my sins in
for a whole year until
the Day of Atonement.
I once asked Mike what
sins he went to confession
to confess. He didn't say.
I once asked Anthony what
sins he went to confession
to confess. He didn't say.
But I knew what they were,
at least what one of them
was. It was the same as mine.
But mine was the only one,
and after a year, masturbation
wasn't a sin anymore, so why

on earth did I envy them when
Mike and Anthony should
have envied me? Maybe they
did envy me. They didn't say.

Today I Saw A Face

Today I saw a face
that should not exist,
a face so beautiful,
so breathtaking, so
heavenly, it should
not exist, but it did,
and all I wanted to do
was fall to my knees
and weep, weep until
the very last tear fell
from eyes that had no
longer any need to see
anything other than
this face, this face that
should not have existed.

How October Ends

Mark it – how
October ends
with a great flurry
of leaves in a hurry
to be done with it
and how the barred
owls, in contrast,
are slow to answer
one another, leaving
the big redheaded
woodpecker free
to fill the interval
with his solitary
tapping, smartly –
Mark it! – upon
the trunk of
the stark oak tree.

A Conversation

"It's not magic, but it's
not miracle, either," Jeff
said. We were talking
about coincidences. "And
they're not coincidences,"
he said. "Okay. Not magic.
Not miracle. Not coincidence.
So what are these mysteries,
Jeff?" I said. "That's what.
Mysteries," he said. "Just like
everything," I said. "No, not
just like everything. You see,
Joel, some mysteries are more
mysterious than others," he said.
That was six months ago. We
haven't talked about it since,
which is no mystery.

On The Road

On the road ahead of us,
a farmer sits on his tractor,
slower than the horse-drawn
wagon of his grandfather,
the enormous rubber wheels
the height of his tallest son,
turning slowly, too slowly
for the motorists behind us,
impatient as always to arrive at
their home lives, real or imagined,
which the farmer has no need to,
which the grandfather could not.

Petunia

Tenacious, obstinate, stubborn,
purple on purpose more
than ever, the last petunia
in the pot leans over the exact spot
the sun was last afternoon.

Conductor

That is what I wanted.

I was eleven.

That was what I wanted.

I asked my father to get a baton at Schirmer's.

That was what I wanted.

I waved it in front of the mirror, the big one in the living room.

I slept with it under my bed.

I carried it to the table at breakfast.

I took it to school in my book bag.

I had pictures of Bernstein and van Karajan and John Barbirolli on the wall.

My father said I was a fool.

My mother said I was a genius.

I didn't become a conductor.

I don't know what happened to the baton.

I don't know what happened to the fool.

I don't know what happened to the genius.

I happened.

That was not what I wanted.

So Here I Am

So here I am, Bill, an old
man speaking of love against
my reason. It is all I can do or
watch a lighter-than-air house
finch feed on the black seed
as though breaking a fast.
Speaking of love learned by heart
long past the loving, at least
you had your river and the means
to cross and the brownstones
and lofts to sleep in there – such
enviable circumstances! – mine
are narrow, limited, confined –-
a prison more than anything –
would it were a garret – waste! –
waste! I am the widower at the window.

It's Good To Be Outside

It's good to be outside
again after days of rain
and cold and cold rain,
again in the warm air,
again governed by a
generous sun. How good
it is to be outside again
among the shadows
sharp on the walls,
sawing through the houses.

Zhao Li

I paused to look at the swamp.

It was silent.

Oh, how I miss my old friend, Zhao Li,

who would read its lips

and tell me what it says.

Nothing Is Approximate

Nothing is
approximate.

The world is exact.
See for yourself

how the world
is as exactly

as it should be.
Nothing is

approximate.
It bears repeating.

No approximation
you can think of

is approximate.
Every sensation

is exact, every
feeling perfect,

every notion
precise. Nothing

is approximate.
Except happiness.

Two Clouds

Two clouds, white as a swan's
wings or an angel's, converge
from the left and the right on
the sun, which lights the clouds
from behind gloriously. Somewhere
someone is dropping to her knees
in prayer, and I, as much as I would
like to, can't blame her.

The Wind Does Not Discriminate

The wind does not discriminate.
The oak leaves and the leaves
of my notebook are one and
the same to it. Why shouldn't they
be? The leaves of the oaks shall
return next year to the oak trees,
and the leaves of the notebook
shall – well, who knows.

Four Things With No Ideas

WASPS

Yes, Bill, but what
kind? I like paper wasps,
those homes they make
out of that ingenious
stuff so much better
than the paper our wispy
poems are written on.

A GENTIAN

Did you have a Bavarian
in your house, Bill, "in
Soft September, at slow,
Sad Michaelmas"?
Did you reach for the same
"blue forked torch" that
Lawrence reached for,
that shed "darkness on
the lost bride and groom"?

OPEN SCISSORS

Why open? Wide
open? How wide
open? I know, Bill.
Wide enough to cut
the poem down to size.

A LADY'S EYES

Bill, why the hell
did you have to say
"centrifugal, centripetal"?

It Is After Noon But Still

It is after noon but still
before evening,
and the indecisive hours rub
off on my hands.

Short November Pastoral

I hear the geese on the lake.
They are speaking of the weather.

I hear the blackbirds in the ash tree.
They are speaking of the weather.

I hear the coyotes across the valley.
They are speaking of the weather.

I hear the barred owls in the woods.
They are speaking of the weather.

I hear my neighbor's chainsaw.
It is speaking of the weather.

Very Short Conversation In The Monastery

Student: "Master,
what is the difference
between having
nothing on your
mind and having
your mind on nothing?"

Master: "Enlightenment."

Neighborhood

There was a church that had
been a synagogue on my street
in the Bronx. I passed it every
day as I walked to Olinville
Junior High School. I would
look up at the star above the door
and up at the cross on the roof
above the star above the door every
time, shaking my head, mumbling,
not believing what I was seeing.
I resented it. I was a Jewish kid,
just bar-mitzvahed, and I resented
that cross lording over King David's
Star, King Solomon's Seal. It got
my goat. I wanted to climb up there,
knock it down and smash it, but
I read some history, not much,
just enough for it to dawn on me
that it made sense. It was logical
for that cross to be up there along
with the star. Shit, it was how the
Christians built their folly on my

people's foundation. I put two
and two together and figured that
the world had become just too much
for the one Yahweh, so He split
Himself into three to oversee it all.
And later, as I looked at the world
so all fucked up with war and famine
and disease and fire and flood, I saw
that it wasn't enough, that three
weren't nearly enough, that He should
have known, that He should have seen
it coming, that He should have split
Himself into ten, or forty, that it was
too late, that I felt sorry for them,
the Father, the Son, the Holy Spirit
who had to beat their three stupid heads
against the wailing wall of the world.

November Morning

The sounds of hunting
get my attention. They
are one sound repeated
over and over, all the
same, each as loud as
the other. There are no
other sounds. If I could
wish a dream upon him,
I would wish him the
dream of being blinded
by the beating of wings,
of being deafened by
the beating of wings,
of being suffocated by
the beating of wings.

Gratitude

Such is
the relief of clouds
that look like nothing save clouds.

Such is
the chainsaw of
my neighbor the best white noise.

Such is
not a flower
to be seen, not a smell in sight.

Such is
the small jet out of
the blue into the blue the one-way blue.

Such is
the sun at
low power the blessing of December.

Such is
the crow that
minds its manners a mensch.

Such is
the notebook
with wide rules and wider rules.

Such is
Glenn Gould's
"Goldberg Variations."

Such is
the span
of dreamless naps.

Such is
the list of
idioms inexhaustible.

Such is
the difference
between anything and any old thing.

Charlie

Mother with her son, Charlie,
at the brewery – no father in
sight – who wants to stand on
the table – and it's Saturday –
says No – Charlie has long locks –
blonde curls like his mother's –
like a girl's – he looks like a girl –
and someday – he – Charlie – will
be – she – and she – Charlie –
will dance on the table all day.

All Things Aspire To Be Round

The square wants to be round.
The triangle wants to be round.
The parallelogram wants to be round.
The octagon wants to be round.
All want to be round to fit, when they die,
into heaven which is round.

The Future Is Female

"The future is female,"
you said, Korkut, so I had
to ask you why. "The future
is female because she is a
beautiful Spanish lady who
comes bringing bad news,"
you said, so I smiled and
nodded and said, "Bring her
on, that senorita, that senora,
for I am ready for her beauty
and for her beautiful bad news."

Miracles

Aren't you always disappointed
that it was not a miracle? Don't
you always hope to see one any
day now? Haven't you heard the
stories from South America?
Haven't you heard the stories from
Africa? Haven't you heard the stories
from Florida? Aren't you sad
that it's never a miracle? Don't
you wish that some miracle would
be true, at least one? That any
miracle will do? That someone
were truly born of a virgin, Jesus
or Dionysus say? Or that someone
actually did ascend to Heaven in
a fiery chariot or on a winged horse?
Or that thing exists, that place, that
Paradise that they ascended to?

Advice To An Old Poet

Just remember this:
Never use the word "fuck"
in a poem unless it's about
a woodchuck you are cursing
out for ruining your garden.
Never use the word "shit"
in a poem unless it's cat shit
and you step in it, but don't
forget to rhyme it every time.
Finally, never use them both in
a poem, for that would be a sin
unless it's the fucking woodchuck's
shit you're stepping in.

Essie

When you apologized,
were those tears in your eyes?

Were those tears in your lustrous brown eyes
when you apologized?

Yes, those were tears in your beautiful eyes
when you apologized.

I wish there weren't tears in your eyes.
I wish you didn't apologize.

There should have been tears in my eyes.
I should have apologized.

Yes, I should have apologized,
but not with any tears in my eyes.

No, no tears that you could see,
dear Essie, dear, dear Essie.

Lunch

I picked up lunch at the Thai place.
It was a beautiful day, the best day
of the year thus far. What a beautiful
day, I said. Yes, very beautiful. Best
day of year. Perfect to go by river
with beer and girlfriend, he said.
I don't have a girlfriend, I said. Oh,
that is sad, he said. Yes, it is sad.
Do you have a girlfriend? I said. No,
I have wife, he said. But it's still a
perfect day to go by the river with
a beer, I said. No, I work here all day.
You go, he said. All right, I'll see
you, I said. See you, he said.

May Pastoral

Hail to you, hummingbird, throated
with ruby, as you sip the sugar water!

Hail to you, jay, plumaged in the blue
of the sky, as you feast on the last suet of the year!

Hail to you, hairy woodpecker,
as you wait your turn on top of the crook there!

Hail to you, mourning dove,
as you softly coo unseen in the wood!

Hail to you, crow, as you carry the cross
of your shadow wherever you go!

Encounter

A barred owl flew over
the road into a tree near
me. I stopped. I looked at
it looking at me. I'll never
know what it saw.

A Pot Without Flowers

The dirt waits to become
soil again, has waited months
in the potting shed's cool dark,
and now, in the sun for the first
time since November's failing sun,
begins to remember what it's for,
begins to anticipate the spade's
plunge, begins to prepare for
the nudging of the suckling roots.

In The Liquor Store

I met one of the librarians
in the liquor store. We both
bought the same red wine.
Going back to work or are
you done for the day? I asked.
Oh, my day isn't done until
six, she said. But it's so sunny
out. So warm. You should go
to the park, sit on a bench,
I said. I wish I could, she said.
Sure you can. Wordsworth says
so, I said. Yes, he did say that,
didn't he? *Up! up! my Friend,*
and quit your books; Or surely
you'll grow double: Up! up! my
Friend, and clear your looks;
Why all this toil and trouble?
she said. Can you recite all of
"The Tables Turned"? I said.
Sure can. I memorized it in high
school, she said. I'm impressed.
Enjoy the wine. You, too, she said.

As Though It Were

made for them,

three finches

sit on a wire.

As though they

were made for it,

three finches

sit on a wire.

Crimson Azalea

Who expected this?
I didn't, not after last
spring's resplendence,
not after such a voice,
so full and so sweet,
with which you sang.
Oh, I hear you, old
crimson azalea. I, too,
am getting old. Old
brother, I, too, am
finding it harder and
harder to force a smile.

No, No, Not

for no reason
nor for any
reason at all,

do I take a
backward glance
to see what

time may emit
there. There is
a reason, one

in particular
that the eyes
know, that the

heart tells them,
for who else
would they obey?

Mysteries

For example, I
followed a wasp
as it zigzagged
across the yard,
curious to see
where its nest was.
It was only one of
many mysteries today.

Saturday

Only men here so far
at the brewery. We two,
two there, two there, only
pairs of men, but it is early,
not yet two o'clock. They
talk about women, their
women, other women, all
women. We talk about
women, our women, other
women, all women. Women.

War

Do we?
Why do we?

Because it is there?
Right there before our eyes?

How do we then?
From above?

From the jet's altitude?
From the drone's?

From the ground?
From the tank's perspective?

From below the ground?
From the soldier's point of view in the trench?

For once, do we not want to witness the triumph of good over evil?
If only for this once?

Big Dogs Brewery

It's in Walden.

It's where the women all look alike.

They all look like the barmaid.

They are all blonde but not good blonde.

They are all bad blonde.

They are all insipid blonde.

They are all dull blonde.

They are all boring blonde.

But she had a personality.

She had a repertoire of endearments.

First it was *sweetheart.*

Then it was *darlin'.*

Finally it was *hon.*

I don't know your name,

so you'll take whatever comes out of mouth, she said.

So I took them.

First I put *sweetheart* in my pocket.

Then I put *darlin'* in my pocket.

Finally I put *hon* in my pocket.

When I got home, I put all three into a glass jar.

I screwed the lid on really tight.

I punched a few small holes in the lid.

I didn't want my endearments to escape.

But I didn't want them to die.

They're on the kitchen table.

I shake the jar to wake them up.

I want to listen to them buzz.

I want to watch them light up like fireflies in the dark kitchen.

They are my very own dear, dear, dear *Dears*.

Wisdom

I am writing outside.
The wind lifts three
or four pages of the
yellow legal pad and
violently shakes them.
"What do you want?"
I ask. "I want you to
stop writing!" the wind
shouts. What a wise wind!

A Butterfly Has

found a marigold.
Then another. And
then another. It has
good taste, for they
are the three prettiest
marigolds in the pot.

Lilies-Of-The-Valley

Yes, they are small.

They are tiny.

They are miniature.

They are found in the Lilliputian valleys.

But they are grateful, nevertheless, that the peonies

are days away from bloom.

Spirea

Small, white flowers,
white first and foremost,
small only after white,
for from a distance, a
cluster is a marigold's
width, so white is its word,
so white is its way in the world.

Work

It calls to me, the work
that needs to be done.
They beckon to me, the
jobs that want no waiting,
the tasks that require my
time. "Come sweep us
clean," say the patio and
the walkway. "Come pull
us up," say the weeds.
"Come mow me," says the
lawn. "Come paint me
already," says the shed door.
"Come wash me for once,"
says the car wiping pollen
from its eyes. "Go replace
me," gestures the broken
birdbath weeping in the grass.

Eleven Dreams

I am driving a convertible
on the Boston trolley tracks
with my brother when it blocks
my way, the sign: *WHO WILL?*

I am late for my poetry class,
and all the students are already gone
except for Emily Dickinson
whose jackboot kicks me in the ass.

I'm on the Bronx train No. 4,
or is it on Air France to Paris?
In berets, the Bronx French curse
because I stand in the door.

A beautiful (So beautiful!) Black podiatrist
examines my right foot. It is blue (So blue!)
and explodes into a blue (So blue!) mist
as she disappears from view.

The conductor with red (So red!) beard and red hair
asks for my train ticket.
As the train jerks backward back (So back!) to nowhere,
his hair turns into a tall black (So tall black!) hat.

The conductor suddenly takes sick.
I leap, swan (So swan!) dive from the balcony.
I stab my right hand with the stick.
It bleeds (So bleeds!) on the violas and the 'celli

I'm driving on a mountain road,
which gets narrower and narrower
until it shrinks to nothing and disappears
into the rock of the mountainside.

I'm a doctor in a big hospital.
I have a stethoscope and wear a white coat.
On the speaker system, there's a STAT.
Everyone runs there but me. I'm not real.

I'm asleep. I wake up. I fall asleep again.
It is morning, but there is no light.
It is morning, but it is night.
The sun and the moon are one.

I am in a kitchen with two sinks.

In one, I wash a spoon. My beautiful wife

in the other, washes a knife.

I look at her. I wonder what she thinks.

I'm in a classroom, in the first row.

At the desk sit a male and a female teacher.

One is a scowling Arthur Schopenhauer,

the other, a bare breasted Marilyn Monroe.

Nearing Solstice

If they don't know,
they certainly are good
at fooling us, the birds,
the butterflies, and all
the rest in their consummate
conspiracy with the sun.

There Is A Yellow

and white Dutch iris

in the garden where

there was never one before,

an interloper among the peonies,

which are just beginning to bow

down from the burden of their burgeoning

behind and to the left and to the right.

Poem Based On A Line By Donald Revell

I do not have a dog.

I never had a dog.

What boy never had a dog?

What teenager, what young man,

never mourned the loss of his best friend in the world?

I was that boy.

I was that teenager, that young man.

I am that old man.

I cannot say that "Death calls my dog by the wrong name."

So I am grateful to you, Donald Revell.

I thank you for sharing your dog,

and I thank you for sharing your dignified disdain for death.

The Restaurant

It's the only poem
on the menu:

Sweet & Sour.
Sweet & Sour This.

Sweet & Sour That.
Soup. Chicken. Shrimp.

It doesn't matter.
Just repeat it:

Sweet. Sour.
Sweet. Sour.

Over and over.
Be slow.

Be deliberate.
Exaggerate the vowels.

The long *ee*
of your sweetheart's kissing.

The round *ow*
of her kicking your shin.

Getting Rid Of Books

We make two stacks on the floor.

The hard covers that will go to the book dealer in Harriman.

The soft covers that will go to the Moffat Library for their book sale.

I tell myself that I will not regret this someday.

I tell myself that I'm not a Nazi, that I'm not burning them.

I tell myself that there is nothing to feel guilty about,

except, perhaps not having read them all.

Nevertheless, I do feel guilt whenever I part with a book,

even a bad one, even one that should never have been

published in the first place.

How exactly did I came by this cowardice,

this vague and childhood guilt

so much like the guilt my parents laid on me when

I left food on my plate while the children in Europe starved?

Poem For Carol

Now. Now is the time,
for courage has finally
caught up with me, so now
the love poem (the only
kind of poem) for Carol
who agreed to coffee
next to her library. She's
the Director, it is hers,
all the books hers, and now
mine, too, in the collection,
except this one, this love
poem the only one of mine
will be for her alone,
at my direction, for Carol.
(O, dear Carol, forgive me,
for this is the best I can do
without embarrassing you.)

There Was Such A Sweetness

suddenly in the air today,

the honeysuckle must have burst

open, poured out its full season

of fragrance all at once,

saving nothing, not a drop for a rainy day.

I Went To The Pharmacy

to buy melatonin. It helps
me sleep. Looking for it,
I found myself in front
of a shelf of testosterone.
There was testosterone
with this, testosterone
with that, testosterone
with stuff I never heard of.
I considered buying one,
not to help me sleep but to
help me stay up. I didn't.
I got two melatonins instead.

The Church

The church here is not pink
like yours, Bill, but white
like all the others, so I cannot
as you did compare it to "the
pink and rounded breasts
of a virgin!" but perhaps to
that same one in her white
wedding dress, tall, erect,
wooden, stock-still at the altar.

Guilt

Today I pulled what
I thought was a weed
up from between two
paving stones, but after
pulling it up, I saw it
had a very small white
flower on its stem. I felt
bad, but is it my fault
that the flower was too
small to see against the
white paving stones? Is
it my fault that I live in
a town that forbids weeds?

Dementia

Sleep is sleep.
All sleepers have one face,
but that sound from the other side,
that sound that sounds like pearls chattering
or Rosary beads breathing,
that sound is the grinding of teeth.

This Afternoon

This afternoon,
the heat built up,
brick by brick, sun
baked, story by story,
until it was level with,
then over our heads, while
the sky, the blue roof of
the heat, beckoned like water
or like the mirage of water.

Another Buddhist

What is it that attracts
them so to him who
never wrote a poem,
at least none we know
about? Ah, yes, it's what
attracts them to the old
ponds, to the frogs jumping
in, to the plop of the water.

They Make The Sound

They make the sound
of jealousy, the birds
that chatter among
themselves. That is
to say, they make the
sound I would make
if I were jealous, which
I am not.

Word

Old English of Germanic origin; related to Dutch *woord*,
from an Indo-European root shared by Latin *verbum* 'word'.

Confucius: "A gentleman would be ashamed should his deeds not
match his words."
Horace: "A picture is a poem without words."

Unknown: "A picture is worth a thousand words."
Samuel Adams: "How strangely will the Tools of a Tyrant pervert the
plain Meaning of Words."

A 2012 movie with Eddie Murphy is *A Thousand Words*.
A 2013 movie with Jason Bateman is *Bad Words*.

A 1950 musical with Fred Astaire is *Three Little Words*.
A 1976 song by Elton John is "Sorry Seems to Be the Hardest Word."

Karaoke is the world's most mispronounced word.
Sequoia is said to be the most beautiful English word.

So, Solonche, do you have any last words on the word *word*?
Yes, and as a poet, I'm a man of my word.

Completely

If you think about
it that way,

meaning completely
(if any thought

can be completely
thought) you

will see what it is,
even, perhaps,

also what it is
meant to be.

Side Effect

She said the medication gave
her a nightmare, the worst,
the most horrible nightmare
she ever had. She said she
should have read the small
print before taking it, but who
reads that tissue paper full of
small print? Really now. Who
does? She said the pharmacist
should have stuck a warning label
on the bottle: *This may give you*
nightmares, the worst, the most
horrible you'll ever have. I said
she should have asked him for the
antidote, the drug that gives you
good dreams. Anyway, what was
the nightmare? Oh, I've put it out
of my mind, she said and hung up.

I'll Wait

As long as I don't
have to say what
I'm waiting for,
I will wait. Shit,
I'll wait 'til Hell
freezes over.

For R.A.

True, many may have
written better poems,
but not one asked
better questions than you.

White Peonies

We wait.

When we go out,

we look to see.

When we go by a window,

we look out to see.

We wait for them to open.

But they do not wait to open.

They are opening,

opening more slowly than our willingness to wait.

For D.G.

First, let me tell you
the review is going well.
Even quoting "Darwin
Never Knew" in its entirety
it will be the right length
for the magazine. Probably
I'll end it with the conclusion
for how it resonates in the mind
long after: "… there are still
dreams inhabiting facts."
But you have to agree there
are still facts inhabiting dreams.
I'm also thinking of quoting
"Tribute" in full, the poem
you chose for the back cover,
which is not only a tribute
to one particular poet, Robert
Bly, on hearing of his death,
but a tribute to poetry itself,
to poetry with its "tall trees
swaying overhead," with its
"nails underneath."

Peonies Long Dead In A Vase

You would have gotten
rid of them long before now,
strewn the burnt brown
petals like the ashes of a loved one.
That I have not, that I still
leave them in the vase to curl and shrink,
tighten into fists striking at nothing,
has nothing to do with you.

Short June Pastoral

A helicopter flies over the lake.
The bald eagle whistles for a mile.

A butterfly alights on a dead peony.
The dead peony lights up.

The wind breaks a branch.
The tree doesn't care, for it has many more.

An ant brings a crumb too big for the entrance.
It finally drags it down but doubtless dies.

A crow with a damaged wing flies above me.
The blue sky shows through the missing feathers.

Three hummingbirds make mayhem at the feeder.
It's a microcosm of mob fitness, ruby-throated.

I Met A Former Student

I met a former student.
I didn't realize he was
until he told me he was.
He and his girlfriend were
in my English 101 class.
They were into heavy metal.
They wore black leather
jackets. They wore chains
and steel stuff all over, but
still I couldn't place him.
"My girlfriend had fiery red
hair and really big boobs,"
he said while making the
really big boobs gesture in
front of his chest. "Oh, yeah,
I remember. How are you?"
I said, extending my hand.

Overheard Overhead

Someone else could have
told you what it was,
helicopter or small private
plane, coming over the trees
beyond your sight, someone
with an ear for such things,
but I know only that whatever
it was, plane or helicopter,
it had no business way up there
in the place Nature promised
to only the birds.

Sonnet Of Memories

Did the dog chase you down the alley?
Did he have a black circle around his right eye?

When you were fourteen years old,
were you in love with Miss Rheingold 1964?

Did you look for her many years later?
Did you find out she had died?

Did you write a letter to Robert Graves on Majorca?
Did you really expect him to answer?

Was the Catholic church made of white stone?
Were the white stones so white they hurt?

Did you pass out in her Brooklyn brownstone?
Did you wonder about your umbrella?

Did you look for her many years later?
Did you know? Did you know she played Nora?

About the Author

Nominated for the National Book Award and Eric Hoffer Book Award and nominated three times for the Pulitzer Prize, J.R. Solonche is the author of 38 books of poetry and coauthor of another. He lives in the Hudson Valley.

Made in the USA
Middletown, DE
13 September 2024

60398241R00064